Peregrine

2021   Volume XXXV

Black Poets Speak

Co-Editors	RACHELLE PARKER
	JAN HAAG
Managing Editor and Layout	JANET SUMMERS
Publisher	AMHERST WRITERS & ARTISTS PRESS

Copyright © 2019 Amherst Writers & Artists Press, Inc.
ISBN: 9798475175262
ISBN 13: 9798475175262
ISSN: 0890-622x

Amherst Writers & Artists Press, Inc.
P.O. Box 1076
Amherst, MA 01004
Phone: 413 253 3307

peregrine@amherstwriters.org
www.amherstwriters.org

Peregrine is published annually. Submission details are available at
amherstwriters.org or peregrinejournal.submittable.com. Payment is in
copies. The editors endorse the practice of simultaneous submissions.

Copies are available on Amazon.com for $12.

Amherst Writers & Artists (AWA) affiliates offer writing workshops for
adults, youth, and children across the world. In addition, AWA sponsors
public readings and maintains an international training program that
supports the work of writers and artists. Amherst Writers & Artists Press,
Inc., publishes *Peregrine*, books of poetry and fiction, and the Amherst
Writers & Artists poetry chapbook series.

Cover art by Barry Moser (used with permission)

Peregrine nesting sketch by Karen Buchinsky (used with permission)

Kim Brandon's essay on denise h. bell first appeared April 19, 2021, in *The
Operating Systems 2021 National Poetry Month Series* on medium.com. It
was curated by JP Howard. Reprinted with permission.

Gretna Wilkinson's poem "1973-2020: George Floyd(s)" was previously published on theravensperch.com. Reprinted with permission.

CONTENTS

This issue of Peregrine, the Amherst Writers & Artists annual journal, Black Poets Speak, is special and important. It is honoring a squelched voice. There are millions of stories to be told by all the millions of people in America. These numbers include Black poets like me offering our stories, memories and legacy to America. It is the beauty of a community's vernacular and syntax. It is talking about our hair's journey to acceptance, gifts from our ancestors, and mothers going mad with worry about their children being killed.

We all would do well to look to the poems here by my poet friend denise h. bell, "daddy's seeds" and "quan according to catino jones / a duplex." The simple use of the name Quan is brilliant. It immediately shows timeline and place. Widely published, bell's poems are a conversation of old men on a park bench fussing about marrying a good woman or their own obituary, a woman having a government job and having a son who is a menace or one with so much promise or not being able to have a son at all, a barren womb. She gives us so many ways and so many voices to consider Black lives. We eagerly put our ear to the wall and listen. My poet friend inspires those around her to do the same.

denise knew how passionate I am about the vernacular and syntax of Black voices. She often wondered, out loud to herself, "Rachelle, are you thinking about leading a workshop?" She would rattle off a list of poets for just about any idea you had or after reading any poem you shared. Always giving and always asking, "What are you working on?" or "Anything new to send me?" She would want to know, after reading one of my poems, "Where're you sending it?" Not if but where. Always with tips. Always polishing her bops and sonnets. She will always be the Queen of Craft.

denise h. bell became an ancestor on February 6, 2021. I am missing her, and no doubt so do contributors Kim Brandon and Shalewa Mackall. Included in this anthology are their poems and an essay each wrote not long after denise's passing to describe what she means to them. She means so much to Brooklyn that a bench in Fort Greene Park is dedicated to her and a banner printed with "Poem about Denise Bell" hangs in her honor. All will agree that denise was the greatest teacher because she was the greatest student. I certainly agree with Kim: "She was so super cool."

Somebody, somewhere asked or wrote about being asked or wrote in response to being asked something like why don't Black people write about flowers? This makes you think that flowers are relative to an individual, relative to a people as success is relative to an individual. We all must define it for ourselves. denise h. bell shows us what flowers are to her as do all the other poets in this special issue of Peregrine, which features some of America's best poets.

—Rachelle Parker
Co-Editor, Black Poets Speak
Amherst Writers & Artists

KIM BRANDON ON DENISE H. BELL

denise h bell (1947–2021) was an extraordinary poet. She passed away in February 2021 after complications from COVID-19. Her poetry is now her voice. Her first collection of urban poems, a crown of sonnets entitled, psalms along myrtle had been completed at the time of death. denise devoted her life to studying the craft of poetry and using it with a laser-like precision to showcase the stories, the hard truths and the sweet victories of marginalized and disenfranchised people. She encouraged and inspired writers to go deeper, to be fearless, to build our own tool boxes and to stand in the fire and then write the poem.

I first met denise h bell at a Women of Color Writers group reading in Brooklyn. She carried herself with a quiet softness. Her poetry on the other hand was raw power. There was realness, a reverence, relatability to each poem. She put in all out there; everything about us and our loved ones. The themes weren't pretty and still she captured the tender humanity of living on the edge.

Kool Aide Epistle

by denise h bell (an excerpt — the last stanza)

i don't know what stopped me from screaming
yo sister i didn't sign up to live on a tight rope
have mercy every day i pray for a better life
i deserve the same love respect you text about

When I was kid back in the 1970's, we lived in a 20-family building. One day someone robbed and murdered the milkman in our vestibule. His body stayed there for hours waiting for the coroner. Anyone who left the building saw him there. This didn't define us. But, it changed us all, none of us for the better. This is how I learned about death and being trapped behind a curtain of poverty. Somehow, the folks in our building leaned into each other. There was a tenderness to our lives that is often invisible eclipsed by despair, judgments and stereotypes of the hood.

When I heard denise h. bell's poetry, I felt at home. I felt that tenderness. I knew these people, we were all locked in or locked out of our dreams and on a rare occasion a body might be the demarcation blocking the way. Her poem Bitter Words speaks to the patches of love and sorrow with her signature precision. Tinderbox nominated Bitter Words for its online poem of the year award in 2017

Bitter Words

jerrod wasn't planned
love kept him growing in my womb
my g.e.d. r.n. was for him
i gave him things i never had
kisses hugs hearing i love you every day
jerrod was never a regret

he makes me forget my once bitter life

jerrod loves art
that's how i got to know a basquiat from a monet
he taught me programming french
jerrod isn't perfect
i'm his drill sergeant
they'll be no numbers under his photo
i don't know why/when/how jump shots became my nerd's passion
jerrod loves manning up/playing with the big dogs

he makes me forget my once bitter life

what you mean Jerrod laying out on the court
they mistook him for who
blood of my blood drained gone no no no
lord jesus jesus lord how could you curse my womb
i can't get this bitter taste out of my mouth

jerrod's gone i can't forget my once bitter life

denise encouraged writers to be fully engaged and not to a poet on the side lines. She was a proud member of Brooklyn's Clinton Hill community. The bullet-less violence of gentrification gave her work a heightened agency. She was involved in many writing communities. She attended Cave Canem-workshops; she was also a Brooklyn Poets fellow; a proud member of Nickle Bag Women's Writers Collective, Women Writers in Bloom Poetry Salon, Women of Color Writers group and others.

Her work appeared in Rattle, Tinderbox Review, Rigorous, Quail Bell, Anti Heroin Chic, The Chaffey Review and many others. denise's poem: "remember my name," was nominated for the Ploughshares Poem of the year.

remember my name

after i retired
i started a routine
discipline won't let my mind wander
every morning i buy a paper coffee
look at obituaries taped on joe's barbershop window
i like it when their families use photos
pictures make the dead more personal
i walk to my bench
watch workers waiting for their bus
they're who i used to be
i was a thirty year transit man
i was union
fought for security dignity
my phone always rang
i was part of the next best thing
retirement made me a used to be
cora's out saving souls
there's no sense in me sitting in an empty house
she prays i stop being stubborn and walk in her light
i watch joe open up
i look to see if he taped up new notices
if he do
i get up read them
while reading i got to thinking
when my when time comes
cora got to put a picture on my obituary
it'll help people remember who i was
the old man that sat on the bench

The Village Voice described her work as "strong, emotional, and proud." her work was in off shore journal, live at the nuyorican café, and the chaffey review. denise's work focuses on the disenfranchised and those who are forced to live a marginalized life. I'm including this link to "a BOP," to show her mastery and dedication to craft.

You can hear denise, reading I AM THE SHIT AKA USED TO BE / A BOP. From Rattle #62 Winter 2018.

Almost three years ago, denise and I both joined Nickle Bag. The group met monthly to support writers over a certain age and to workshop together. The goal was to complete a writing project. Denise was well on her way. She had her manuscript in the final stages and was simply looking to get feedback on her pieces before publishing her collection. The women in Nickle Bag were a gift to me. We met monthly to offer support and critiques.

This was when I noticed the extreme dedication denise had to her craft. The sonnets, the sestina, the villanelle, and the Zuihitsu forms were her playground. She studied form with the best poets. And read everybody and said her favorite place was Poets House. She said that poet Georgia Douglas Johnson was her spirit guide.

She was very private except when it came to her love of poetry. Here she was open, generous and non-competitive. Her advice to me was to stay true to my voice, first and foremost and then she advised me to read far and wide, find poetic voices similar to mine. She heard more Lucille Clifton, Sharon Olds, Ai in my voice. Funny how we are the seeds of other poetic legacies and don't always know it. Lucille Clifton and Ntozake Shange are my spirit guides. They appear in my poems like old friends.

denise suggested I join more serious workshops and retreats — like Cave Canem, VONA and Wild Seed. She introduced me to Brooklyn Poets, where I would join her two years later in the honor of being a Brooklyn Poet, Poet of the Week.

She suggested that we all submit more work to top shelf journals, apply for fellowships and awards, and we did. As she reviewed my work, she sometimes suggested playing with structure and trying the poem in a different poetic form. For the most part she simply encouraged me to "keep doing."

There were always "check this out" emails from denise. Nicklebag moved a to daily action/accountability thing — via a text each morning. It was amazing to see all the work she put into her being a poet. This more than any replicated into my own writing life. I completed my first collection — Red Honey and submitted it. I became a VONA alum, attended Wild Seed and a Cave Canem workshop. I am fully engaged in my Brooklyn writing communities.

kiesha's blues

smoke the pipe let me dwell in my so called deep thoughts
foggy poisoned thoughts built a monument to my mind
a mind that rationalized a strange sense of values
a mind that began crying why me what now

smoke the pipe built a sham lurid monument to my mind
a mind that's drowned in k2's frustrations ferocious fears
a mind that could no longer ignore vicious truths

i didn't want to listen see hear truths
truths replaced smoke pipe illusions brought about by them
i'm doomed my new reality screams
unlike jesus you won't be risen to a new life
face it baby you're doomed to dwell in nothingness

caused by your addicted scrambled fried brain bullshit

———

denise told of a dozen ways to die on the avenue and just who would be left to grieve. She showed us just how much love could be found if only you know to turn your head to the side a tiny bit and shake loose all that bias you were taught about certain people. I came to see that it was well worth it — as love in times of sorrow — if far sweeter than any other.

I wrote this poem Out of Sight with denise on my mind — here is an excerpt.

out of sight...
each year our number of smiling visitors
declines a little more
so do our phone calls and the care packages
while the line at the men's prison is standing room only
I keep meaning to ask other Black women why this is
I don't I'm too afraid to hear that me being in here
means they're doing time too
I listen to the long timers
they say you can either do your time or the time does you
I focus on my appeal, my safety and my sanity...

denise's work impacts my poetic voice. She changed the way my narrator especially in "I" poems. My goal is to remember the richness of knowing that we are all victims trying to be heroes, and villains missing the mark of becoming saints.

This was denise's ARTISTIC STATEMENT:

I write poetry because it is my initial way to relay my despair, empathy, compassion, and passion. My poems focus on those who are marginalized because they are poor, aged, mentally ill or victimized by the oppressive behavior of so called "normal, run of the mill people."

I use many poetic forms when I craft my work. I am quite intrigued by the Bop, Sonnet, Persona, Duplex, internal rhymes and alliteration. I believe poetry is more than jotting down words. It is a craft that demands listening, reading, studying, writing, and rewriting...

vashti's lament

i so wanted to have a womb bearing fruit
i so wanted him/her to suckle from my breast

when i was young i so wanted an almond joy
my daddy's best friend gave me my favorite candy

all i had to do was to sit on
daddy's best friend's lap
he his hands began to poke hurt me

once i so wanted to teach my womb fruit to read write
i'd show him or her nothing but love

grandma was washing my panties
she screamed how you get them stains
you too young to menstruate

daddy came home got his glock
he blew aaron away
the judge set daddy free
cause he suffered temporary insanity

grandma said daddy was right to kill aaron
to this day
daddy walks around frustrated fighting mad

me i don't have no more taste for almond joy
i'll never bear fruit in my womb
i'll never be able to give him/her my love

There is so much more to denise h bell. This is what I came to know in our time workshopping together. If I can be as passionate about my family, my work, my community as denise was, then I can count myself as one of the many writers she helped to flourish.

So just how do you say goodbye to a warrior poet friend sister? You don't! I am committed to sharing her voice and her brilliance.

This essay first appeared April 19, 2021, in *The Operating Systems 2021 National Poetry Month Series* on medium.com. It was curated by JP Howard. Reprinted with permission.

SHALEWA MACKALL ON DENISE H. BELL

Today I remember a new ancestor, the poet denise bell. We became friends in a Cave Canem workshop. She encouraged my writing and reminded me of the importance of not always being the elder friend in multigenerational friendships. denise shared her favorite poet, Georgia Douglas Johnson, with me.

As soon as I looked up her work, I instantly recognized the title of one of Johnson's most well-known poems as the title of one of Maya Angelou's memoirs. I also recognized her community making with the S Street Salon--where for more than 40 years Georgia Douglas Johnson hosted literary community in her home--as an antecedent to my two most beloved poetry communities, the Women Writers in Bloom Poetry Salon created and curated by J.P. Howard and Poetry & Chill launched by Leslie McIntosh. denise attended WWiBPS gatherings and P&C emerges from relationships forged in the very workshop where I first met denise bell.

May denise #RestInPower.

May denise #RestinPeace.

#GoodnBlack

#BHM

#BFM

daddy's seeds

i should have yelled
daddy speak up
demanded he tell me what he mumbled
when he came down from his high
if i did my life wouldn't be a living hell

every february 2nd
i open my baby samantha's memory bag
i take out her what would been her baptism dress
hug her gold cross jordan and i brought
as a praise and thanksgiving to our god
that gave us a child to love

all the time i was carrying you samantha
daddy spoke what i called mumble jumble
once he stammered i'm to blame for you and jordan's sin
i thought he spoke gibberish after smoking too much weed

i kiss samantha's cross
that was supposed to bring me and jordan continued bliss
i cry   samantha your father is running the streets
screaming raging full of regrets   shame
your daddy is drinking sniffing   shooting up
wanting to find a someone man enough to kill him
i should have demanded what your grandfather mumbled

when he came down from his high

baby girl during your fifth month in my belly
i began to get sick
my mind's eye kept asking me why wasn't i feeling right
i went to doctor washington
he took scans
made me and jordan swab our mouths
he b.s.ed me saying he collected all of his patients dna
i fell for his lies
your daddy and i went to get our results
i shouted doctor washington
no way can jordan and i can sister and brother

baby girl
i should have made your grandfather repeat what he mumbled
when he came down from his high

samantha i had to do what was right for you
i gave you back to jesus
i didn't want you laying in a crib
not seeing hearing
being fed by tubes
i know you are sitting on his right hand side

your grandfather's clean
the bible is his guiding light
he begs me to forgive his sin
your daddy's soul is lost
his humanness can't be found

i pack samantha's bag
place it in my sacred place

samantha have mercy on me
i'm trying to find the courage   strength
im too shattered i can't take out your memories
another year

quan according to catino jones/a duplex

quan met shorty to get him a gun
that piece was to protect mama and him

quan's piece was gonna protect his mama and him
my boy bopped down the street fearing no man

my boy bopped down the street fearing no man
quan was always feeling kissing his gun

my man be always feeling kissing his gun
his momma knew nothing about his new piece

his momma knew nothing about his new piece
miss kay turned her troubles over to the lord

miss kay turned her troubles over to the lord
quan never really knew how to handle his gun

quan never knew how to use his gun bang he's dead
he shouldn't have met shorty to get that gun

Sit Here for a Word

Sit here for a word,
they say
and memory
undiscovered trickles in
a cool wind
glides across my cheek
a rocking as if
on a gentle sea
heralds their message
mostly: Keep going
and listen to us
with your whole body

Will you comply
this time?

Plug into a river story
flowing from a waterfall
unseen
a swirling blackness
that you know is home

I am still being born,
my ancestors say,
still opening my eyes

Help me bloom this life
into flight
unfurl like the shape
of sweetness

Remember

The poets see things
others want to
disappear
or forget
like bodies stacked on trucks
moving quietly
after midnight
or forged documents
to make a child a wife

We remember for us all
the head-on collisions
of who we perform
and what we really be

We can see
the bottom of the glacier
in new moon sea
and the cracked cog in the
big machine

We feel the electric charge
in the air that spins itself
over great distances
into thunder, lightning
revolutions

We sense the confusion
that creates runaway egos
turned leaders turned despots

We urge you to

STOP

Listen to the
strumming of the threads of life
that weave us into a wave
a being
that is no less separate
than water

We want you to
remember who you are

We are
a star

Abyss

Black death on cue
is a canker mouth
wrapped around
a straw grafted onto your spirit
and you can't/won't see
how the grotesque drinks itself into existence
through you

Some abyss belly
consumes you
makes you residual
belches back
a flat reality
of trinkets
that trick the eye
into believing
talking cadavers
called president, prime minister, premier
leave you wondering why
you always the after
thought

Not a march
not a law
not a god
can cut the feeding tube

Just you

Ahmaud

from spring pavement cracks
corona of coverup
summer reckoning

Breonna

the downpour of hail
blows violent from the breezeway
mare falls uncovered

George

a last wisp of air
returns to its mother tongue
and the reign descends

No Matter What Happens, Don't Move

My father gathered us together
his children
Then gathered up all the rusty dented
leftover cans of house paint
from the floor of the hall closet

> He heard them first
> before we saw them
> the police were coming again
> this time
> their sirens raging war
> breaking small fragments
> of peace found on the poverty line

Popping the lids off
like flipping pancakes
Them smelling like turpentine and burnt offering
Him, pouring them over us
his children
heavy globs dripping over us
coating everything below
our crowns
and our new and hand-me-down clothes

He put his index finger to his lips to silence us
His eyes pleading
be still my children
be still

> The door pushed in
> He was knocked down
> punched
> kicked
> Guns were jammed into his face
> He—handcuffed
> and dragged away from us

The paint dried

We had not been seen
Had not been discovered
We are now the same baby blue from bathroom walls

and the same canary yellow from the kitchen walls
and the same soft butterscotch gold from the living room walls

Safe and invisible
for the time being
as long as we don't move.

The Coming of the Lord (Ultima Pars)

The Lord had said in his very final days,
My blood, my spirit, has rained down,
down on all the folks, an entire country.
You will see, o humbled men, ye sons,
you will see, daughters, young and elderly,
and you will dream, even you who wore chains
and were called no citizens, no men, nobody.
You have my soul and spirit, all that I gave,
so you will see all, your fate, America's destiny.
Cast your heads up, and look upon the canopy
that lights whole worlds, blazing stars, eternally!
Then look down to the banner of your fathers,
the flag of your mothers, generation after generation,
for in both, I will place the divine signs to gather
their hemorrhaging flame and ruined smoke, a nation
driven to the earth's wallowing dust down below,
to dark space will turn the sun's deep-white glow,
and under night's black coat I will drive a moon
upon her blood-auburn rays, a sign clear and true.
All this in more star-bright omen I will do to show
that indeed it was the Lord who had come to you,
the one to free all men, so all hearken that ye know!

House of Slams and Hollers

For Iley Jordan

who occupies those storefront houses at the crossroads
shotgun houses like abandoned churches

       one house slouched behind the musty aroma of trees

windowsill radio chatters like a bird on caffeine
the living room smells swampy with ashes and bottle caps
kitchen of vintage graveyard-shift coffee, boiled viceroys,
cicadas with exoskeletons of brandy
and chickens chained in the backyard

night turns over haunted with moths

air cooled with shuffled decks
and howling hounds missing hell

the methane of certain ghosts
gets drawn like window shades
dealt in   poured shots
at this place where the road crosses its legs
       like a gentleman

here lies the uncharted territories of some blues::
stigmata blues   razorblade blues
blues for lips just out of reach
blues screaming blouses of plaster down bedroom walls

choirs of apocalypse blues ignite the red wicks of their tongues
sing harmony to calm bluegill river
for Saturday's baptism of hot lead

dawn rises with fire on its mind, takes off its top hat

names smile from his mouth in comets, false crosses

anything not already on the ground
    holding on, praying
done grabbed a guitar, a shotgun
      and ran

Heirloom Noodles

He and I share mothers,
but entirely different creation stories.

Three Fridays after she died
we meet for dinner at a mirror-walled restaurant;

its dervish of steaming platters,
noodles taffy-pulled at the door—

This feels like an affair I want to kick away from

but he's the only one remembers me
　　　as if my life really did happen.

I don't like who I am with him.
We both should be different.

We—neither of us—will speak in honest diagnoses
of soured rooms,　　　　the body's dark indifferent magic

how breath, sometimes, will leave a path of bruises

or how people frost & drop off the vine while you watch them
your hands clean, pocketed.

Having buried one mother already,
I know this territory—

my hands salted from 100 nights of fever.
　　　A brother should tell another what's coming
as much as what's been.

I've rehearsed this meal for days now
but after sitting with him, I forgot my line.

We play catch with silence & trivia

A crash of salt thumps the edge of his plate
rimshot to the corniest of jokes.

The awkward intimacy between men—
How we punch the confines of our closest embraces.

My Body Is a Litany

i am hostage to ancestry—born knotted with memory
forged familiarity ladder stitched into my dna

an invisible lineage of nitroglycerine adorns this blood
my skin a mirror forged from sand smuggled across time

there's a perpetual calendar outcropped down my spine
its ignited marrow   sizzling

i am a bone clock of 10,000 hands dap pounding
through a championship of former seasons

my body chimes their names
its river of capillaries murmur the syllables

i am tattooed with the family bible,
                tongue and all

a litany of names each one an ember
burning the skin map it touches

all ghosts dressed in flames belong to me
i am their wildfire of voices, singing

It's Raining on the Moon

It's Raining on the Moon,
Not a cloud in the Sky.
The only Clouds visible are rolling under the Golden Gate,
riding with total respect on the spirits of the Shell Mounds.
A slither of the Moon is seen in view,
45 degrees to the Western Horizon.
While Rain Falls on the Moon,
Clouds forming in our Hearts,
these Clouds, called Whether Cloudz
Tempered by our intuition to manifest the weather in our Life
Whether Cloudz, the Clouds that protect the Spirit
of the Land and Molecular Beings to reside on it.
Many shapes, dances with the wind,
Flashing Lightning, setting off a Drumming Thunderous Applaud
the Energy of the Clouds, so Miraculously tantalizing.
The colors go deep into the Universe,
look up, see there, the Whether Cloudz welcome you.
Whether Cloudz reflect the best in us.
The Reflections reflect on you, "Shine."
Not a Clouds in the Sky can stop you,
reflect on yourself.
Whether Cloudz are always reflected in and around you.
the transparent aroma of the Clouds gracing the lands.
The Whether Cloudz, says, enjoy my fragrances that I have gifted you
    with.
The Wind is calling, the Whether Cloudz to the next Land of
    Cloudiness.
Let us Dance into the Sunset, to places Whether Cloudz gather,
to protect the Planet Earth.
Breathe, Feel, Feel, Breathe.
The Cloudz are Beautiful,
while it is Raining on the Moon

SHELLEY JOHNSON CAREY

The United Nations of My Hair
An Uneasy Alliance

To reveal unknown DNA,
I bestow a gift unto myself.
Puzzle pieces from times gone by,
My heredity of stealth.
Genetic markers in a vial,
Mailed to the land of *Who Am I?*

Born with tresses dark and thick,
Smoothed by amniotic pomade.
Locks now white but disguised to conceal
My youth-chasing charade.
Coils colored bronze, red, or plum,
Or as gold as my sunset yet to come.

Though three-fifths citizen memories remain,
A hope for insight lingers.
Dark to light, black to white,
Like question marks through my fingers.
Emails then arrive bringing answers to my prayer,
Clues to decode the age-old mysteries of my hair.

Ancestral paths that intersect—
Congo, Nigeria, Cameroon,
Norway, Ireland, Spain—
All witnessed the Middle Passage moon.
And flowing down my back are waves
That lulled to sleep captors and enslaved.

Britain versus Benin, Sweden versus Senegal,
Diasporic clashes in the land of cotton.
Stolen roots tinted and styled
To mask memories not forgotten.
Ringlets that cling to my hairline's nape
Guard coercion secrets and children of rape.

My legacy of massive curls,
Wrap around time and place.
A blond girl/black man amalgam,
Tap, tap, tap a tune of race.
They Bojangle down my double helix,
To an R&B and country music remix.

But despite the disruption of my genes
By Union Jack's colonial forages,
Neither the stickiest gel nor flat iron's sting
Can flatten my nappy edges.
My resolute strands of rigidity
Bloom in fevered humidity.

Whispering chants from the Motherland,
These warriors frame my face.
Kinky wisps, proud and free,
Rise high to claim their space.
And triumphantly refusing to be bowed down,
They form my magnificent African crown.

Promise Please

Jericho

I
No name for nut doll
Takes time for old but new
Become familiar on tongue
Hold it
Stroke it
Sit with it
Understand its Mojo.

A thrift-shop score,
She clutches a fierce satchel,
Aspirin tin painted black,
Hard flowers, glass beads strung
On rusted wire.
At threshold,
I boomerang to save her
Dixie-feet, which hitched
To Adirondacks.

No name for doll rocking
Southwest Indian print dress
Chills with ten Made-in-China Pocahontases.
Odd doll out, all priced $15,
She waits for freedom
Presses black-velvet in jewel case.

No mind doctor here
No veiled seer stare
To decipher why nameless doll
In brown-traveling shoes
Invokes visceral joy or hate.

II

The New Testament Jericho
Sprints like a wide receiver
Across Hawkins Hall
Put that away!
Get that away from me!

How does a post-Civil War to Depression-era
Artifact with a walnut visage,
Eight-ball eyes, red lips and grinning teeth
Make a Shreveport native son Bojangles?

What is the why and how of a doll
Made by long-ago hands
Deep below the Mason-Dixon?
It's easier to make the Mississippi wine
Than walk on words
Or name a doll powerful
As Laveau.

III

A California poet
Adorns her Westport home
With doll parts—porcelain heads and limbs—
Discombobulated bits
Suspended in glass vessels
Centuries of offerings
A strange love.

Jericho labels Doll Coven
Women of the word, by the word, for the word.
All fear the XX child
With text-looping DNA
Rescuers of abandoned dolls.

Beneath the last-quarter moon,
The "National Treasure" ferries
Across shining waters.
Anybody who loves that doll has no
Understanding of the mysteries of the Universe.

Atlanta, Emory and Ebola welcome
Black Poetry Day Poet back home
Nut doll waits in an electric-blue sack
For a name.

gravity

on the tv the astrophysicist says that if we pack too much into one *space? time? thing? is like a star?* instant of a place we may create a black hole and I think of data like the scratchings on a table or the entries of the thin encyclopedia or the flapping CD the thumbed drive even how we make our body need with emotional density and I see all that *information? data? stuff?* as if it were a pancake pressed and flattened to be petted on its head a gentled coddled kind of fiend limbs just itching to grope remember grieve so here I change the channel finally because stone tablet or CD or drive is only an emptiness that that sifting astrophysicist flirting just a bit I think with the chair of the physics department never talked about and I want the meat of it well the taste anyway the spice the singing how it feels the way of my daughter's hair coiled into my fingers with my mama's voice brass a snare in the background of each of my memories or this even the writing of it the flat page and raised typeset rushing always to condense its secrets outward and weren't you astrophysicist lady only supposed to be explaining gravity how it holds and makes us connect each thing to the other to the next for I only wanted to teach my daughter something simple *we can watch something else baby* not her grandma hardly able to rise from the bed too heavy and pressed with pain to grasp onto me comb my hair bend me backwards all around her and how much I wanted that layer of her hands pressing my scalp where I can just shrink down forget the explanations like why I always hold on so tightly to the hard stuff why I always fall so fast and full of what has happened or better what is happening swapping position greedy because that lady smiling at that man is right it is inevitable this little girl's life in my own full of my mother's own and the thick of it information and stuff only to be collected like fingerbones muscle stacked layered unseen

Displaced Persons, 1951–Now

Mother pushed me, sort of preemie, to school.
Not kicking or screaming, but docile,
No stranger to paper and pencil,
I then sat, a careful only child,
Among dozens of pale curious eyes,
Their bloody star, even, destined to rise
Above me, more feared than fearless,
Born the wrong year—odd, just shy of peace.

Did my babble and pitter patter tire her?
What did Mother aspire to or fear
That pushed her to push me? Under the radar,
My ghost twin, her stalled soprano height
Entangled my song. Skipped—darkly bright,
At school—then put back by life's dull weight.

***

Eleanor M took first prize in fourth grade but said
"I won last year. I cheered for you instead."
Altar boy John T—bad girls snickered sissy—
Spent his last school picnic tickets—the Fun House?—on me.
Catherine S of the dark soft pageboy and bangs,
Little Miss America poise with rich girl things—
Did she hop-scotch with Jane C, spoiled "only" like me,
Cleaning Our Lady's steps each morn on bended knee?
Lone Lithuanian Nancy N begged me bring
Halloween Newborn to school—Can't hold back Spring!
Ginger Paula M, apartment-bred, asked me—surprise!
To the last all-girls birthday party of our lives.
By sixth grade's end all had passed me by.
Giant green dreams had enchanted them away.

*In the 1950s and 1960s, seven Roman Catholic churches with large
parish schools reached their zenith at the southern end of West
Philadelphia: St. James, St. Francis de Sales, Transfiguration of Our
Lord, St. Carthage, Most Blessed Sacrament, Good Shepherd, and
St. Clement. By the year 2010, because of their declining White
congregations, all were closed, consolidated, sold or demolished.*

The Smaller Facts

Last night on the northbound 52 Bus
I overheard a woman reminisce
"You know Woolworth's at Market…"
Then drifted off her flotsam voice
Across the aisle, yet cutting quick
My silent rosary chant, a public
Transit muscle I flex against
Profanity, insanity, and inanity.

Mighty red in the Sixties under the somber
Shadow of the El, Woolworth forever
Owned that West Philly corner—or
So it seemed to me, a child (then teen)
On brief excursions with (then for) Mother
To buy such and such, this and that, an order
Of existence so routine, thought to have been
A creature, not of craft, but nature.

In uniforms (sniffing the "Bandstand" caste?)
Pearly Catholic girls sold dime store taste
Like trusties in a prison commissary—
My 17th summer, this so ordinary
I never tickled the manager's door
For a job—Me, a darkie daughter
Of the faith crowned with the gold stars
Of Distinguished Honors.

Woolworth's gone, a species not extinct
But evolved. Entanglements dissolved,
Here and there the family name intact.
And this transitory stranger, younger
Than me, probably, with her cropped Afro…
Fifty years ago, I did so, too.
Without her terra cotta tint.
Revolution pruned to a smaller fact.

*In 1960 Woolworth's in Greensboro, NC, was the site of the first lunch
counter sit-in of the Civil Rights Movement. The building is now a
museum. "Rainbow," a clothing store, currently occupies the 52nd
and Market Street Woolworth's site in West Philly. In 2020 the police*

teargassed the mostly Black-owned business strip after looting disrupted days of peaceful demonstrations by Black Lives Matter supporters.

Forfeiture, Not Civil

Called home by one left feeling not free,
I stood stunned in my late childhood backyard,
Now mine. Gone, the May roses and trellis.
Too much shade from the unpruned family tree?
Then I tramped through invasive ivy where
Clover had once rambled among the grass.
A sight worse than this foreign weedy spree
Stopped me at my yard's shared iron border—
My nameless elder neighbor in distress?

Vine-smothered humps in the yard. Treacherous
Back stairs. Black-eye windows. Off-the-hinge
Shed screen door. Caved-in roof. Shingles askew.
Horror movie set? Scared? Curious?
Left-behind hearsay made me cringe,
More than fire and bugs—But crime like the flu
Fell on others, right? Not meticulous
Us. "Cops caught the dope son selling. No binge.
Momma lost her roof." "Poor credit?" "Can't sue."

Philadelphia's civil asset forfeiture policy pulled in millions of dollars
per year and seized thousands of homes and vehicles as a tool of the
"war on drugs." In 2014, the Institute for Justice sued the city as one of
the nation's worst examples of civil forfeiture overreach.

Some Say Glory Is in the Living
I Say Glory Is in the Surviving

Black women have always
excelled at survival
We learned how
to chew up rocks
and spit out a smooth
enough cement to make
a steady road
We've always made do
with less
Grabbed what we could
with nimble fingers
We ate less than our share
Used our hungry mouths
to pray for better days
Our bodies
Our beautiful Black bodies
have always been bridges
for our children
for our men
for other women who could not
bear the whip, sting or lash
This time is no different
Even as they try to extinguish us
we live with such a mighty breath
climbing out of our windpipes
it sounds like a brass bell's ringing
to remind the Ancestors
of our living
Our fingerprints are indelible
on this greedy landscape of America
we call home
Beware
Beware
Beware
When the levees break
and the waters rise
It is a Black woman who

learned how to breathe
underwater all along

The Fabric of Our Lives

Since today is the day of rising
We can feel free to surrender
ourselves to ascension
At night when we lay
our heavy heads
on fluffed pillows
we wrap our bodies
in white cotton sheets
in anticipation of sweet slumber
In our dreams
Our Ancestors greet us
They give us prayers, songs, recipes,
lottery numbers, healing herbs to swallow
for when we make it
back to our bodies
Praise to the ones
who share our faces
Before they release us to our waking
They say no matter how much
we pay for fine garments
silk and peau de soie, ashoke or lace
It is the cotton that they sacrificed for,
It is the cotton that they toiled over
It is the cotton that they imagined
a better life for us over
They say wear it,
wear the cotton proudly
resist in it
prosper in it
Be free in its woven threads

Within

If I know nothing else
I know a Black Woman
must keep a reservoir
buried deep within her gullet
A hidden space
to store slivers of daylight in
Steal away
Steal away time for yourself
Black Woman
Add what you need
to your body
Nourish your spirit
with long forgotten dreams
You don't owe nobody
nothing for your survival
Let them wonder
Wonder how you keep
finding your way
through the darkness
There are people who hide
patches of midnight
in their pockets
hoping to drop you
into a black hole
never to be seen again
This is when you use
your magic
Unhinge your jaw
Open your mouth wide
pull that daylight out
of the recessed part
of your woman self
Blind them
Escape
Thrive
Begin
Live

JESSICA LYNN DAILEY-KEITHLINE

Mama and Son

In the moment that I heard him call out for his mama…
The reality and the fear and the gravity of being your mama became
    real
It became tangible.

The realization that my gorgeous, giggly, sometimes solemn little boy
exists with a short-lived innocence
because in a world where White Supremacy exists,
Black Boy Joy is hard to come by
and Black childhood is a very limited time lease.

One day the charm of your smile
the wisdom behind the eyes that we share
will be outweighed by your tall stature: strong arms and heavy hands
your kindness ignored in lieu of fearing your body.

I look at you and wonder when
the crossover from adorable child to threat begins:
8, 10, 14?
The youngest person to ever get the electric chair was George Stinney,
convicted of murder after 10 minutes and an all-White jury.
Emmet was also 14. Trayvon 17. Tamir 12.

When will folks begin crossing the street to avoid you?
What age does Black boyhood end?
Does it ever really begin?
In the moment, I heard him call for his mama
I heard your husky voice,
You call for me when distressed: hungry, scared,
bored with the scenery of your playpen.
To you, Mama is the management and file your every complaint with
her

In the moment, I heard him call for his mama—writhing, crying,
    begging.
I realized how wrong my own mother had been
She said membership in the Fraternal Sisterhood of Black Mothers
was a lifetime gig

In a world where lynching a Black man in the street
in front of his community and friends
cutting off his air supply with hands casually rested in pockets

as if it's just another day
humanity does not extend to darker hues

We live in a place where an empty-eyed Sandra is propped
against a wall for a mugshot
long after life has left her body—in a world of that sort,
Black motherhood is a job that extends even after I leave this plane
and go to the next.
In that moment, I wanted his mama to come reclaim for her child
ending the close to 9 minutes of torture,
she left nothing but a corpse for the demon of desecrate.
I imagine her lifted from her resting place to tend to the cries
of her 46-year-old baby

In that moment, I knew that not even death ends
the cover a mother gives her child.
In that moment, I knew the day you were born I was enlisted
I had signed up both intentionally and unintentionally
for a job that will follow me into eternity.
This is forever.

And should you ever call for me, know this:
I'll show up just like his mama,
and you and I will burn this down together,
hand-in-hand, Mama and son.

JESSICA LYNN DAILEY-KEITHLINE

Chocolate Mabbie Grew Up/Reflections Over Fish

*And he said unto my light-skinned friend: "OOOhhh, Gurl, you so pretty
and light skinned."*
—*Outside Jesso's, Oakland, Calif.*

I am content to be the dark shadow haunting the corners of your eyes.
Ignore me if you will/I am the reminder of the ugly, disdainful
    Mammie
Not a favorite amongst Massa
No remix of the original/Regular Black

My hair has not/will not/wants not to flow down my back
Wool-like without a relaxer, alteration/I prefer myself without
    ornament
Your love for these mulatta mamas/admiration for the mixture
This will not affect the way in which I see me/Black reflected in your
    eyes is falsehood

Oakland, formally the cradle of Black advancement, elevated thought
Now no further from the colonized mind than anywhere else
No talk of the colorism/Black-Black girls hope to catch a break
We remain in the shadows of forgotten ignorance

Now on the verge of extinction.
Ignored, under-appreciated, mama-like, ugly
I bask in your ignorance. I am the ugly root
I hold you to ugly history. I am strength through darkness.

JESSICA LYNN DAILEY-KEITHLINE

Three years and four pregnancies

Four times I have wet white sticks waiting on matching pink lines
Four times I have suffered weeks of nausea and food aversions,
vertigo and shifting organs
Three years and four pregnancies, resulting in two babies.

April 25th marked the last time.

Last time I would count kicks and wear paneled pants.
Last time I would panic waiting for the daily thump of fetal
    movement
Last time I would test the rhythm of prospective names off my tongue,
        writing each in cursive to see how it would look on
        monogrammed blankets

This was the last time I would hold tight to my miracle secret until
a heartbeat is found and   scans are cleared.

There's absolute resolution in acknowledging the finale of the body's
    work
towards motherhood.
My fertility was a hard-fought battle.
This charming little boy with his boundless energy and
tenacious little girl with her curious eyes and delicate features
        are proof I won the war.

This is the end of an era.

I recognize, accept and hold close the pain of my angel baby losses,
        remembering each time they were scraped from my womb
I remember how determined I was to replace each with new,
    thumping life.
There is beauty in my 50/50 odds, beauty in the baby girl that rounds
    out this show.

Three years, 4 pregnancies and 2 babies.

I am accepting the finality of closing down shop.
She is my last breath on two and push on three.
        Time will no longer be measured in months and belly
centimeters

The curtain has been called.

This is the last time.

The Birthing Chamber

(Inspired by an article WPLG Local10.com, May 8, 2019)

You could hear her screams
subhuman worse than a black bear
caught in a steel trap
recalled an ear witness
to eye witness news.

An abandoned Black woman pregnant,
bipolar-schizophrenic tethered
to a jail bed was in labor.

See, this is how they treat us.

The ear witness told story with back to camera
said never again ever would she want
to see what she saw and hear what she heard
the day a prisoner gave birth alone.

They thought Tammy was oblivious to pain
after her addiction to self-medicating cocaine,
the howling patient shunned and shamed.
Guards insisted *Crazy Black women don't feel pain.*

See, this is how they did her.

The woman's womb broke open.
Old caesarean keloids stretched and wept
labor's cruel tentacles pierced and pinched.
Help! she shouted, pushed and squatted 7 hours:

Baby coming. Baby coming now. God, it hurts.
It hurts, please, please, please, somebody, please help me
Uh, uh, uuuuuhhh, oh God, it's coming, help us,
please, somebody have mercy, please, help me, oh Jesus!

Sympathy pains punctured nearby vaginas
inmates in cells recalled their own birth agony,
wept with Tammy, screamed for help but jailers played
sadistic roulette with mother and fetus's health.

See, this is how they did them.

The blood-splattered birth chamber
resembled remnants of a Santeria ceremony
in the Divided States of America

a nation quilted in hatred
where even a dog gets more mercy.

Miranda fell from her mother
hit the floor and wailed; with palsied arms
Tammy cradled her bloody, mucous-covered baby
and whispered: *Mommy is so sorry.*

I Learned About America

I learned about America
in the daycare
where babies
of revolutionaries
cried for
their mothers
to hold them

I learned about America
in my grandmother's house
where I was held
with bedtime stories
nighttime baths
and desserts
on weekends

I learned about America
In 1982 when the revolution was over
We woke to an old, soiled mattress on our front lawn
and a pair of dirty sneakers hanging from the telephone wires

The kids down the street wanted to fight me
because I was the new girl in their raggedy old neighborhood
They acted like it was my fault—
>   our small, dirty houses were built too close together
>   a drunk mother came home and stabbed her teenage daughter
>   pedophiles preyed on little girls getting candy from the liquor
>   store

They had no idea my parents fought for
them to have free breakfast in school
>   neither did I

I learned about America
in the secrets my parents kept
not knowing where to begin
Don't tell anyone
we were in The Party

I learned about America
in the tinge of resignation
in my grandmother's voice

when she said she was voting
for the lesser of two evils

And the matter-of-fact way
she explained
white flight
redlining and
we live in the ghetto

And the way she didn't blame
us for what America is
Those boys wouldn't be hanging on the corner
if The Panthers were around
They'd have something to do!

I learned all about America
by the age of 10

We live in a blue house with flowers in front in Lefferts Garden

why this color, the stutter of sky ocean and twilight
the ancient Egyptian use lapis lazuli for heaven
and if Mary is sad on the façade of this headline
this mishap on a busy intersection, opening the news-
paper, see the resurrection, two daughters left on the side
of the highway, Domini, five, and Dioni, three, when does

pure blue come from spirituality, I can see the pajamas
hooded down coats wearing UGGs boots, disposable
diapers left to refresh when the police asked she said,
my name is Domini and my little sister is Dioni
feel the color of sapphire, ask the muses for mercy

with this heighten power, begin to weep as I
continue to read their story, turquoise keeps me
calm, so I will not worry, then the oldest said, "My mom's
name is Dalisha." It is the power of color, so maybe they
can reach her, the little one continues by saying, "We live
in a blue house with flowers in front."

Statue

She climbed atop of the Statue of Liberty to Protest injustice.
A bust of nude Amazon women, fingernails chipped like
razor wires, she is a fire alarm, born of the Congo, a mom's egg
fled from Staten Island with placard and tape, make it a ballad

of tragedy, madden by this future, fussy over her children
for she is eminent domain, as plain as liberty, not a cotillion
adorned white, but milk and breasts are tests as she scales the body
her reckless and naughty ways she climbs rocks, find it a thrill

until she becomes a threat for she knows migration as an abolitionist
geography, first it's the base, her tongue becomes mace
if you refute her, if you exclude her, if you disturb this piece
the incitement will increase as the crowd look up, but it's a bust

and a beat down, until she turns around, the sound is of a trance
as she takes this stand on a man's soapbox, carrying a placard
as she tried to reach the mansard roof of her mouth in which she
screams and flails, the tufts of her hair become bales of cotton

all the world weighs her shoulder, but liberty contains mold, a sort
of cesspool green in patina, as the police takes her, they pull at her
seams or the hem of her dress, she is no less vital than Alice Paul
or Fannie Pankhurst, a purse of insurrection, without protection
  clause

she is no less that Mary or Shirley, Hillary or Lilith, she wants to
  reach
the pillbox hat, the crown, the founding of the nation, she cries
creation, a nation of mourning, turns her head for the people;
for it is green not blue any word will due.

Ode to Santa Barbara

on the corner of Ocean and Wilshire
there stood this woman as erect as obelisk
her hands fold as suffragette
but we call her lady

we call her sister as she looks towards
the hill with salmon pink carnations
thrown at her feet for she is the holy see
not a seeker of fame but seer

her way was the only way out
if we want deliverance she does
grant forgiveness if bold enough
to face the sea, and plead with

her possible moment for she
is divine, a holy believer
as I call her Fatima, Guadelupe
the Lady of Malibu, or Harriet

sojourner as child I call her
we ate goodness, Grandma
fed the fullness, she would stay
until the end with
our broken bends, weep
for the sick and shut in
for the soul to keep

then look to the sunshine
the only lifeline.

Their Lot

The black loamy hole dug for her,
the one everybody said was her place,
her lot: How do you fill a hole
when you stand at the bottom
muddy waters rising up.
You grab hold of whatever
you can, especially if it looks solid
like something you can stand on.
Something that just might
hold your weight.

All you have is a fistful of prayer.
She'd outgrown the steeple game,
hands-clasped, fingers locked inside,
turned inside out, wiggly fingers
were the congregation.
She had no time for a faith
that wiggled and squirmed. She
needed blessed assurance.

The preacher said *build on solid rock;*
She said *Amen,* rose to her feet,
arms stretched up; her open hands
felt a change in the air, something
touched her. *Up above her head
she heard music in the air.*

Her uncle, the one who stepped up and out
to Chicago to play black ball, in the game
where only the ball was white, preached
a different resurrection sermon
*Own your own. A man can stand tall
on his own land.* Standing his face into
the hawk, he bought buildings,
not much to look at, but when he climbed
to the roof, he stood astride the city of big shoulders
its streets and yards at his feet.

She and her man bought a little
piece of land, not even an acre.
The deed they signed called it

a lot. This little piece of land was
their chosen lot. When flood waters
rose, they knew what to do to raise
their lot above the muddy waters.
Dump truck after dump truck
of river sand until their lot
was land they could stand on.

A Found Poem of the Former Confederate States of America

We pledge

To be rather than to seem
> Like-minded confederates
> Who in *friendship* swear
> *Thus always to tyrants*
> Big government and Washington over-reach

We dare defend our rights
> State rights to our peculiar institutions,
> Our lost cause and battle flags,
> Our monument avenues

We declare
The birth of a nation where

The people rule
> Not dark-skinned foreigners
> In a foreign land they call home

With wisdom, justice and moderation
> With all deliberate speed
> As molasses flowed on proclamation day

While we breathe, we hope
Ready in soul and resource
> To fend off audacity and uppity-ness
> Dam mighty streams of righteousness

In God we trust
> O, vengeful God, we are your tribe
> Dedicated to *agriculture and commerce*
> The harvest of cheap labor

Union, justice, confidence
> Forever just us

By valor and arms

State Mottoes:
North Carolina: *To be rather than to seem*
Texas: *Friendship*
Virginia: *Thus always to tyrants*

Alabama: *We dare defend our rights*
Arkansas: *The people rule*
Georgia: *Wisdom, justice and moderation*
South Carolina: *While I breathe, I hope/Ready in soul and resource*
Florida: *In God we trust*
Tennessee: *Agriculture and Commerce*
Louisiana: *Union, justice, confidence*
Mississippi: *By valor and arms*

No Rights Which A White Man Is Bound to Respect

"[African Americans] had for more than a century before been regarded as beings of an inferior order, and altogether unfit to associate with the white race, either in social or political relations; and so far inferior, that they had no rights which the white man was bound to respect...."

—Dred Scott decision, 1857

No, you can't
Don't do that

No, you won't
You can't go there
You can't be here

Don't sit there
Don't drink here
You can't eat here

Don't look at her
Don't whistle
Don't look him in the eye

You can't work here
            do not apply

You can't buy a house here
You won't be my neighbor
Don't be seen here after sundown

You don't belong

Don't question
Don't speak up or talk back

Don't kneel
Don't move unless you are told
            to do so

Don't reach for anything
Don't expect anything

Don't try to be
Don't say your life matters

Tarot Reader

A fair table is set. All the relics of her trade are in their proper place.

Her hourglass is there to remind us that time continues on, and the pink sand slowly falls.

Each grain is reminiscent of a decision that must be made before our time completely runs out.

Her crystals glisten as a small ray of light enters, an otherwise, dark room.

Her black cat paces back and forth as if to mark the territory where the reading is set to begin.

A simple glass of distilled water sits to the right of the center of the table.

It is so placed to give life to the reading.

The scent of Frankincense and Myrrh engulf the room.

Alas, the tarot reader breaks the eerie silence with the clearing of her throat.

She shuffles her cards, and each one yields to the pressure of the shuffle, then falls.

It will be a five-card spread: Ace of Wands, Chariot, 5 of Swords, Tower, and Sun.

Her eyes search the cards.

She clarifies, "It seems there will be some disappointment, quick movement, a gift—your final outcome, the Sun."

Satisfied with the reading, I placed a bill in her cup, pulled back my chair, and made my way to the door. A quick left, then a right, I was heading in the direction of my destiny.

JACQUELINE LITTLEJOHN

Migrant Worker

I look at her way out in the distance. Her silhouette looks worn and tired as she works the field. She picks something round, maybe oranges. Her basket overflows with a harvest that belongs to someone other than herself.

There are other women, but my eyes remain fixed upon her. They pass each other but they dare not speak. Frivolous chatter will only translate to money lost so she quickly moves along. She only stops briefly when she needs to straighten her aching back or readjust the wide straw hat that protects her face from the burning sun.

So many rows of fruit left to pick. At first, she wildly snatches the low hanging fruit, then she decides to change her strategy. She stretches her arms as if to reach the heavens. She was not picking fruit, she was praying.

Heaven Is Full

He spent all of his days trying to do good. His family adored him, and his neighbors did as well.

He loved the children. They all called him Dad. He didn't mind because he loved being a father.

His work was always with purpose, aiding the sick, feeding the hungry, clothing the poor. A rare and beautiful person, his plate was always full.

He grew older, and his good deeds became far fewer. He did them with love.

He just didn't know how much longer he could do them.

Then one starry night the Creator whispered in his ear that his work on Earth was done.

A final prayer and a good man was gone. As his soul ascended into the heavens for his final run, a sign rested peacefully at the gate, which read, "all the rooms are taken, heaven is full."

HEATHER LOBBAN-VIRAVONG

Whiteness

It's like snow that sticks to everything
Clinging to the side of tree trunks,
Branches and leaves hanging low
Such heaviness, even the grass
Cannot raise its white tips.
Yet I must clear a path and
Lift the burden until my arms
Are familiar with the motion
Hoist and throw, hoist and throw.
Never one with the snow
And yet there you are.

Dear Daughters

Although I never birthed you
I have loved you
known you
claimed you as some part of mine
from first sight. Sometimes
we meet in my classroom
more and more often we are colleagues
collaborators. In any case
you shine and I see you. Then I see me
in you, and I know—we people:

sharers of a belonging to
and a coming from; singers
of hard harmonies and dissonances
caught in crowded corners of stuffy rooms;
keepers of the sacred ways.
Mixtresses keyed into formulae spelled
out in line-sung hymns & Cardi's rhymes,
turnt in ring shouts & sticky-floored ciphers,
consecrated by take away plates
loaded for the journey with extra
pie and sweet tea in styrofoam.

We churched in our own ways.
The rising up of blue notes, set free
praising the Holy Ghost or caught up in Spirit
like folks flattened by downing fifths
be a lineage. We unbroken from before
Ma and Bessie, me and you
both. Daughters of these women
who found and named each other
beloved, who laid some part of themselves out
across the rocky ledges and busted curbs
to be a soft place for sister-
sharers of the road as they walked it
into being for us coming up
behind. We people. Anointed from birth,

nod acknowledged, embraced.
We people, in full. Blessing theirs

we know our hearts. Full with love
magic and mortal delicacy, daughters
always know, we people. Never forget
Black girls, we people.

Mississippi Barbecue

Postcard #80 from "Without Sanctuary" exhibit

Sliced away and soaking
  in jars, the sweet parts:
      tongue
      eyes
      genitals   saved
  for luck and souvenirs.

The negro ablaze   back
arched as if in ecstasy.

Having lingered
  once too long
on a white woman's face

he is reclined
      bullet-ridden   languid
on the blistering pyre.

Centered in the tableau
still-life posed for
the cameraman's steady eye.

Twice   the magnesium
      flash sparks
through the dapper crowd:

two score fedora & bonnet
crowned heads
  lean into sightline.
Swamp-rot
  and blood-lust crawl
through the eyes.

Later   there's potato
salad & sweet cold tea.

Soaked in blood   soaked
  in piss   the hunting sack
crumpled into itself
at fire's edge, smolders.

Rumor is the postcards
will be a dollar.

The body
now chalking toward pristine
is left to the children

its grin
crackling in tinder.

The Sheriff's
                youngest boy
        rattles a cane 'round
the ribcage 'til it caves
        like a miner's tomb.

A fiery halo
blossoms on the chin.
Bits of charred
        flesh flake away
        float lazily
on the night breeze.

Flame-struck and
        spellbound
the pastor
    sucks absently

a rib-bone   prays
    the children understand
the need
        for cleansing.

Glass

I vowed
   never again
to cross that street.

But the snake charmer
   laid his flute
along my spine.

Sodium light
   painted
my shadow crooked
   across the restaurant's
      plate glass

my breath quickening
against the pane.

Inside,
   mint teas
   incense
   dark spices
tinted air.

A belly dancer
timed finger cymbals
and a coined sash

to a *baglama's*
      dulcet strumming.

      Hand-woven
tapestries
      thickened the walls

tugging
at connecting studs.

Couches crouched
      low and sensuous

every divan and ottoman
                  adorned
with scented pillows
and entwined legs.

She and I were
  only here once

I reminded myself.

Still, the music pulsed
the glass
        beneath my fingers

as hookah pipes
            rose and fell

like empires,
  like longing.

Nomads

For six days we purify metal,
sleepwalking through sulfur clouds.
A few pennies forged with every muscled
clang of pig iron and rust. Friday's
whistle, our Pavlovian call to bedlam,
triggers us down to dogs.

Come Saturday, we hang our checks
on new shoes, silk ties, gold chains.
Scrub iron ore from our fingers,
coke dust from faces before slow fading
from day to night. A bottle of gin
passes between us. We stiff-leg and
hip-drop a pimp down the boulevard;

tug our hats down until our faces
are curved horizons with brown, felt
suns rising askew. Walking the bricks,
we crave music worth killing for:
manna soaked in bourbon, grilled
over hot Mississippi coals.

The *Easy Lion Jazz Joint* exhales
an intoxicating vibration
of wood-stomp and tremor-slide.
Bass so cold it shatters hot breath.

The sax man's vibrato wrenches
moans from our bodies,
sways us into fevered cattails
wrapped in sweat and silk.
Spit-shined leather begins to fly.

Two more juke joints before sunrise.
A plate of ribs and a whiskey sour.
Sunday morning is a hangover
hard as an I-beam stove into our heads.
All too soon, the factory whistle.

ELISHIA PETERSON

At Least Two Pairs

She just wanted to be loved
to the sounds of Biggie and Biz Markie
tape rockin' then poppin' from side A to B
She wanted to show love not hate
gold rings and Radio Raheem tings
bamboo earrings, at least two pairs,
spelling out JADE
oh how they flocked to see her
she used to dig the brothers with a fade
other people's money made her sing
falsetto like, BK ghetto like
on Broadway, the water hose on to the max
imagining it was a giant wave
float on out the Stuy
or maybe for now
soar on the stoop
with her soulful stereo on blast
orange soda in her cup
as she turns the music up

Your Body is Meant for More Than Dying

Your body is meant for more than dying
Your lips are dry and cracked at the corners
And you rub Blistex over them
And it stings
But in a slow burning way

Your eyes open
And you're lying on your back
On the hood of a car
And the sky is turning from orange and yellow
To a fuchsia hue with plum shadows
And it is the most beautiful sunset you have ever seen

Your ear twitches
To the sound of your baby's first cry
There's sweat on your brow and you are exhausted
But your baby is born

Your nostrils flare
As you breathe in deeply
To take in the smell of your favorite dish
Made by your grandma

The hairs on your arm stand up
As your lover trails their fingertips
Down your spine
And kisses your neck

Your heartbeat quickens
As you zipline across a rainforest
Somewhere tropical
Your skin is warm and darkened
From the sun
The air smells different when you're on vacation

Your hands are sweaty
As you move a tassel from one side of your cap to the other
And you dry them off on your gown

The music is loud and vibrates through your body from your feet
As you dance
You spent an hour fussing at your twist out

Only for the sweat to send it in a frizz
But you feel free

Your mother spent months thinking of the perfect name for you
One that would gain adoration but also respect,
was youthful enough for a baby and wise enough for you to grow old
    into
Not for it to be a speck on a list/a hashtag for a T-Shirt/
a chant at a rally to be yelled and yelled and yelled
until it no longer mattered why the yelling started in the first place.
By people who don't know how much you liked to dance/or travel/
or that you have one dimple that only showed when you laughed,

Your lips...
Your eyes...
Your nose...
You...
Your body is meant for more than dying

numb

lights out and candle flick you moonlight from your stomach the
empty room crush your black body limb apart from limb. smoke
waft from blunt and incense and sage and candle and you don't
know which smoke your lungs carry, how many smokes can your
lungs carry? you being evil spirit try to burn out yourself there is not
healing in your hurting. the smokes snake around your face but they
are no mask. you see you. no cracked mirror can see what you can
see without a reflection. ash the blunt and flick it out the window and
when you are heaven high you smile and think yourself gorgeous
like stained glass and rayleigh scattering and laugh and dance in
the mirror, not cracked, thumbprint smudged. when you low like
fangtooth viperfish territory she be left to bask in flooding fury
feeling feelings that feel like feeling and feeling dont feel so fucking
fair. but nothing does the trick quite like feeling it all. black bodies
burning at a pulpit and God says the abominable will rise and ashes
scatter and holy is thine skin curdling under heat like milk. skin like
milk is beauty is eyes ocean like blue is lip pink salami thin is straight
pasta like hair is. it is. and ugly like big butt is skin earth like dirt like
eyes like soft hair big shape moon like blackness unless it is white.
and who decides who deserves to die?

Ode to the Women of Black Lives Matter vs. U.S. Law Enforcement

Analogue to "Ode to the Harlem Globetrotters vs. The Washington Generals" by Kevin Young

Because you never shirk.

Because Trayvon Martin.

Because for you, political will
    is literal.

Because by your mouths
    your necks, shoulders,
      & feet, the world can change.

Because our body
    on a rope.

Because wrongful executions of innocents.

Because our blood a government beverage.

Because who else meets a cocked glock with
    a bared chest.

Because the best offense
    is a bald-faced truth.

Because rage, not just sorrow.

Because the tide
    of our insistence breaking
    on their silica heads

turns their hard, hateful corpus to dust.

Why Did You Kill My Father?

Since Daddy's death,
Saturdays had become our day to shop
or, in most cases, window shop. I dreaded it.
Made me sick to my stomach. It was a ritual, though.
I remember Mom parking Blue, our four-door Chevy
on Westminster Street in downtown Providence.

We got out of the car.

Mama spotted someone who made her nervous.
She had trouble finding the key to unlock the car,
but she did. "Get in, girls," she said, "hurry."

We obeyed—no questions asked.

"Lock your doors," Mama said.
"See that cop over there?
That's the cop who killed your father."

My first tattoo. His face in my mind.
Light skin, blue-green eyes, pudgy face
like a bulldog, his face seared into my brain.

I was walking home when I saw him
sitting in his police car, the windows rolled up.
I'd been at the library, viewing microfilm,
trying to find articles about my father.

I was 8 and felt lonely and empty without him.
The flowers on his grave hadn't even withered.

I walked across the street, tapped lightly on the window.

He smiled and rolled it down.
"Hi, little girl, how may I help you today?"

Without bitterness in my heart, I politely said,

"Yes, officer. I have a question.

Why did you kill my father?

Why did you not just take him to jail?"

I waited for an answer.
But he wasn't smiling anymore.
He turned his face away from mine,

rolled up the window,
started the car, drove away.

I asked him myself, I thought.
And he had no words.
He had no words.

Some things are not in a day's work.

Looking back, I'm proud of that child.
She lives within me. Still the same.
She forgives easily until she's had enough.

Daddy played a part, too.
He didn't deserve to die at the hands of anyone.
Life is not ours to give or to take.

Looking back, I know I changed that officer's life.
Daddy was gone, but perhaps the officer
would never do that again—

I know I helped that man.

Praise the Undeniable Black Woman

her palms crisscrossed with empires,
her mother tongue Mali, Gao, Ségou

Hair twisted like threads of Amazons,
elbows pointed ends of darkened palaces

Each toenail the necropolis of queens
Each knee-cap well-formed & gracious

Her ear's helix is tattooed with slave seed
but her heels grind that common threat

In each armpit there be venerable cities—
& like a panther, her nose protects them

Amidst her eyelashes, a reign of years
stretches across the long jumps of sand

Her ass is the Seychelles' archipelagos
Her smile arcs—gloriously—through time

babypink

I asked the girls to go to brunch because my girlfriend's sleeping. They said they were busy. My ex-girlfriend called. She asked if I knew the name of the bar we broke up in. I didn't. It smelled like hard times, cherry Coke, and men with wives at home who know their names but not the colors of the rooms they built in their mind castles where they're safe and sound. Their Eagles jerseys begged their favorite football players to be still, for once, and listen to their pain. They held hands, bowed their heads, and said a prayer. "Fly Eagles fly." I took a selfie in the bathroom. Someone etched "You'll never learn," beside the tattooed mirror, and I wondered if men speak an untranslatable mother tongue. Does "that was clearly offsides," mean I miss my father and I wish we had gone fishing more often? Does "this ref's taking bribes," mean I wish I was bigger? Does the idol worship fill the hole she chiseled when she left? I wonder

If the girls are busy, I read *Watchmen* while my record player croons Ella Fitzgerald. I light six grape blunts and smoke them, watch my girlfriend sleep, and pray she feels entitled to rooms in my mind castle. We talk, but I avoid difficult topics like the fact that, if I were a Biblical character, I would be Uriah. Men destroy me when they lust for her. Their yellow eyes wander. They wonder how a miniature, 5'5" girl scores such a beautiful woman. They tell me, silently, I do not deserve her. In fact, they put me at the frontline of their devastating war with their entitlement over women's bodies, their insecurities, and their terror that their world's slipping away.

My girlfriend's still asleep, so I go for mimosas. I order huevos rancheros. Some unfortunate lad discovers me and asks to buy me something. I ask him for Pepto Bismol. He gets some and spills it all over his shirt. He's furious because, "What will they think if I wear baby pink?" If I were single, I'd consider him. He looks boring and handsome. Instead, I offer to trade shirts and walk him home.

Gather

Gather the ancients. Gather them to the deep cavernous inward parts. In the silence, hear their whispers, their cries. Feel their stirrings to rise and break every chain. Feel the strength of their truth. Embrace the forebearers' sojourns meant to transcend. Gather them into the marrow of bone, of sinew. Be consumed by their purpose. Negate the spaces occupied by doubt, fear and acceptance. Let the hollowness within, be filled with hope that change awaits. Gather the spirits of warriors, of champions. Gather them like rivers to the seas, where no recompense lies, where the omnipresent yearnings to breathe the sweet breath of freedom floats upon the eternal ebb and flow. Gather their convictions, keep them there until they take hold. Do not falter or wane. Stand up O people. Gather the ancients who lie dormant in the stillness within. When the gathering is done, hold them no more. Plant the seeds of ancestral legacy into the little ones, the in between ones, the aged ones, so that they too will gather the ancients' power and nobility that is rightfully theirs. Let it be handed down one by one for all time. Gather the ancients.

1973-2020: George Floyd(s)

On May 25, 2020, George Floyd, a 46-year-old Black man died in
Minneapolis, Minn., after Derek Chauvin, a white police officer, knelt on
Floyd's neck for 9 minutes and 29 seconds.

in the event i am pregnant, i pray it's not a boy.
dear god half-mighty! the child is constantly
dying in my never-ending nightmares. once,
he left my uterus around twelve years old
fully clothed, taking his pacifier, and
what i believe is the placenta

this newborn ignored my cries of pain
and began unscrewing his own head. mission
accomplished, he unsnapped his neck,
popped his head back on like it was a cap,
cradled the neck with his free arm,
and left the delivery-room

by now, my tongue is parched; and every
word i have ever known is dry-rotted.
she's in shock, the midwife mumbles

with no means to ask where he was going,
i could feel helplessness scorching my palate.
i forgot to worry if i would ever see him again.
for i did not name him, obeying
Dead Black Children Anonymous motto:
if mothers don't name our babies, we stand
a better chance of not losing our minds,
becoming arsonists, or mass murderers,
or dying before our time

finally…finally…*Maammmaa!!!*…the wail
broke free from my throat and shocked
the first shock out of me. i wanted my dead
mother resurrected. maybe Mama-power
could find my baby still holding his neck
and turn his body home to my bosom

you'll know him, Mama. he's the handsome one
protecting his neck. hurryhurry! tell him about
the Birds & the Bees & the Men in Blue.

The Three B's, Mama. Tell him straightaway.
Theresnotmuchtimenow...there's n...o...t
Mu....ch   t...t...i___ Maammmaa!!!

CONTRIBUTORS

Keisha-Gaye Anderson, M.F.A., is the author of *Everything Is Necessary* (Willow Books, 2019), *Gathering the Waters* (Jamii, 2014), and *A Spell for Living* (forthcoming from Agape), named Editor's Choice for the Numinous Orisons, Luminous Origin Literary Award.

denise h bell was a mature urban poet. Her work explored the world of those pushed to life's margins. She was a Brooklyn Poets Fellow, and her poetry was published by Rattle, Peregrine, Antiheroine Chic, and Rigorous. She died Feb. 6, 2021.

Lisa Brathwaite speaks on life in 17 syllables and is the author of a poetry collection *true hotku: 69 haiku celebration of women and our real hotness*. Winner of the 2015 Lee & Low Books New Voices Award, Lisa strives to amplify #BlackLivesMatter through radical demonstrations of Black joy.

Kim Brandon is a Poet/Artist/Activist/Storyteller. Her work has been included in stage performances, anthologies, and journals. She is a Brooklyn Poets' Poet of the Week, a VONA alum, and has attended Wild Seed Retreats and a Cave Canem Writers Workshop. Her first collection, *Red Honey,* is due out this year.

Rob McKeever Bullard is an expert in classical languages and poetry, with an M.A. from the University of Arizona in the classics and a B.A. from Emory University in Latin. His perspective as a classicist influences his storytelling and poetry style; his experience as a Black American influences the content and voice in his poetry.

Oakland native **James Cagney** is the author of *Black Steel Magnolias In The Hour of Chaos Theory,* winner of the PEN Oakland 2019 Josephine Miles Award. Visit Nomadicpress.org for his book. Read more writing at TheDirtyRat.blog

Ron Calime uses wordplay to describe the findings in his photography of social issues, nature, spirituality, and many visions of his camera, he puts them to words. He intertwines stories with his photos, adding beauty to disaster, seeing colors in new dimensions, engineering words with a mind presence beyond three dimensions.

Shelley Johnson Carey studied writing at Hampshire College. She is the author of *Thin Mint Memories*, a celebration of Girl Scout cookies. Shelley recently retired from a long editorial career, holds an M.F.A. in nonfiction writing from Goucher College, and is an Amherst Writers & Artists workshop facilitator.

Robin M. Caudell, an award-winning journalist and Nikki's mom, lives in the Adirondacks. A native of Maryland's Eastern Shore, she is a graduate of the University of Maryland at College Park and Goddard College. A Cave Canem Fellow, she is a Gotham Writers Workshop and Bread Loaf Writers' Conference alum.

Nikia Chaney is the author of *us mouth* (University of Hell Press, 2018) and two chapbooks, *Sis Fuss* (Orange Monkey Publishing, 2012) and *ladies, please* (Dancing Girl Press, 2012). She has served as Inlandia Literary Laureate (2016-2018), founding editor of shufpoetry, an online journal for experimental poetry, and founding editor of Jamii Publishing, a publishing imprint dedicated to fostering community among poets and writers.

First poetry editor at feminist Aphra and Ms., **Yvonne Chism-Peace** received awards from NEA (1974/1984), BRIO (1991), Leeway (fiction/2003), Pushcart Prize (v.6). Recent print: Black in the Middle (Belt), Pennsylvania English (2020), CV 2- Canadian Poetry (43.2), Home: An Anthology (Flexible), Quiet Diamonds 2019/2018 (Orchard Street), 161 One-Minute Monologues (Smith & Kraus).

Janel Cloyd was awarded a Willow Arts Alliance Residency with history concentration in the Weeksville African American Cultural Arts Center. She has been published in *The Black Lives Have Always Mattered Anthology* edited by Abiodun Oyewole, as well as in Raising Mothers, Mom Egg, Poeming Pigeon, Cave Canem Digital, Gathering Round, Peregrine, and others.

Jessica Lynn Dailey-Keithline is a writer, mother, and wife. She was inspired to write at a young age when she found her mother's journals and letters and listened to her father's stories. Jessica believes in the power of using one's voice to dispel ignorance and fight for freedom.

Angela M. Franklin is a writer, poet, and documentarian from Los Angeles, CA. A recent M.F.A. graduate from Antioch University Los Angeles, she volunteers with Pongo, a poetry-writing project for teens in juvenile detention. Social justice is her passion and muse, which is reflected in her published work.

Meres-Sia Gabriel is the author of the best-selling book *I Twirl in the Smoke*. She coaches writers in the U.S. and abroad with her program "Life-Changing Writing in Eight Weeks: Write Your Book, Inspire Others, and Leave Your Mark on the World!"

Robert Gibbons, a native Floridian, came to New York City in 2007 in search of his muse Langston Hughes and found a vibrant contemporary poetry community. His first book, *Close to the Tree,* was published by the New York-based Three Rooms Press in 2012. Robert lives in Brooklyn and continues to be active in the New York poetry scene. *Flight* is his second poetry collection.

Kate Hymes has led AWA workshops for over 20 years and served on the AWA Board until 2020. Her poems have appeared in a number of anthologies, most recently mightier: Poets for Social Justice, published by Calling All Poets, 2020. She lives, writes and leads Wallkill Valley Writers workshops in New Paltz, NY.

Jacqueline Littlejohn received a doctorate in educational leadership from Kean University in 2014. She is currently executive director of a business she formed in 2018 that operates in partnership with the state of New Jersey to service clients who have a developmental disability. She also serves as a board of trustees member, mentor, and soon-to-be published author of a book of poetry.

Heather Lobban-Viravong writes poetry to capture all that is felt but remains unsaid. She is the co-author of a manuscript entitled "Finding Friendship at the Color Line: Conversations Then & Now."

Shalewa Mackall, an artist and educator dedicated to liberatory creative practice, was a 2019 Poets House Emerging Poets Fellow. Mackall, a Brooklynite, Garifuna woman, proud Gen X-er, mid-career choreographer, mother, daughter, cancer survivor, pie maker, and Deep House head, has work published in African Writer Magazine and forthcoming in Obsidian.

Poet Laureate Emeritus of Sacramento, **Indigo Moor's** fourth book of poetry *Everybody's Jonesin' for Something,* took second place in the University of Nebraska Press' Backwater Prize. His second book, *Through the Stonecutter's Window,* won Northwestern University Press' Cave Canem prize. His first and third books, *Tap-Root* and *In the Room of Thirsts & Hungers,* were both published by Main Street Rag. Indigo is a visiting professor for Dominican University's M.F.A. program, teaching poetry and short fiction.

Elishia Peterson is a poet, author, and elementary teacher residing in Brooklyn, NY. Originally from West Philadelphia, Elishia grew up with a passion to share stories with impact. She received a B.A. in print communications in 2009 and a master's degree in writing studies in 2013. She is the author of *Blacklisted: 12 Men Facing Stigma & Success.*

Jhazalyn Prince was born and raised in Brooklyn, NY. She graduated from Hampshire College in 2018 with a B.A. in liberal arts. She is a poet with special interest in interdisciplinary writing and exploring themes of maternal relationships, body image, race, and intergenerational trauma, to name a few.

Michelle R. Smith is the programming associate for Literary Cleveland and a teaching artist for Lake Eric Ink. In 2018, Michelle created THE BLAX MUSEUM, an annual artistic showcase open to all forms and dedicated to honoring notable Black figures in American history and culture. Her second full poetry collection, *The Vagina Analogues,* was self-published in September 2020.

Vivian Dixon Sober has been writing since childhood. She earned a journalism degree from California State University, Sacramento (CSUS) and worked as a writer for the CSUS Foundation. She currently writes fiction, nonfiction, poetry, and short stories. She loves to read and has been writing book reviews for various publications for 14 years.

Lynne Thompson was appointed Poet Laureate for the City of Los Angeles in 2021. She is the author of *Start With a Small Guitar, Beg No Pardon,* and *Fretwork*. Recent work appears or is forthcoming in the journals Black Warrior Review, Massachusetts Review, and 2020's Best American Poetry.

Kaia Valentine is a poet and short story author from Tacoma, WA. She has a B.A. in political science and philosophy, which culminated in a successful thesis on the modern phenomenon of transracialism. She values spirituality, intersectionality, emotional intelligence, and deep dissections of American culture.

Valerie Verdia is a retired registered nurse from Brooklyn, NY. She is an avid reader and writes short-story fiction and narrative poetry. In addition, she is a member of the NY Writers Coalition and the Brooklyn Society Writers Workshops.

Gretna Wilkinson, Ph.D., worked as a missionary teacher in the jungles of her native Guyana. She has authored five chapbooks and one full-length book, *Opening the Drawer* (Amazon). A Dodge Foundation Poet, she performs in the New York-Philadelphia metro area and on the West Coast with the ensemble Cool Women.

Peregrine

THE JOURNAL OF AMHERST WRITERS & ARTISTS

Peregrine has provided a forum for national and international writers since 1983, and is committed to finding exceptional work by both emerging and established writers. We seek work that is unpretentious, memorable, and reflects diversity of voice. We accept only original and unpublished poetry and short stories. No work for or by children. *Peregrine*, published by Amherst Writers & Artists Press, is staffed by volunteers. All decisions are made by the editors after all submissions have arrived, so our response time may be slower than that of other literary journals. We welcome simultaneous submissions.

Poetry: Three to five single-spaced, one-page poems. We seek poems that inform and surprise us.

Prose: Short stories, double-spaced, 750 words maximum (include word count on first page); shorter stories have a better chance.

For additional submission details, please see www.amherstwriters. com or peregrinejournal.submittable.com. All submissions are via submittable.com unless other arrangements are made.

Additional copies of this issue are available at Amazon.com for $12.

The Editors
Amherst Writers & Artists Press
P.O. Box 1076
Amherst, MA 01004
www.amherstwriters.org

Made in the USA
Monee, IL
20 September 2021